I'm Alive!

I Can Move

Written by Mandy Suhr
Illustrated by Mike Gordon

WAYLAND

When I was born
I was very little.

First published in 1991 by Firefly Books Limited.

This edition published in 1993 by Wayland (Publishers) Ltd.

This revised edition published in 2009 by Wayland,
338 Euston Road, London NW1 3BH.

Wayland Australia
Level 17/207 Kent Street, Sydney, NSW 2000

Consultant: Jane Battell

British Library Cataloguing in Publication Data
Suhr, Mandy
I can move.–(I'm alive)
1. Musculoskeletal system–Pictorial works–Juvenile literature.
2. human locomotion–Pictorial works–Juvenile literature.
I. Title II. Series III. Gordon, Mike.
612.7'6-dc22

ISBN 9780750259484

Printed in China

Wayland is a division of Hachette Children's Books,
an Hachette UK company.

www.hachette.co.uk

This book is to be returned on or before
the last date stamped below.

I could kick my feet and move my arms but I couldn't even sit up.

I had to be carried everywhere.

As I grew, my bones and muscles got bigger and stronger.

Soon I could move around on my own.

I can move in lots of different ways now.

I can skip...

run...

jump...

roll and dance.

I can do all these things because
I have a skeleton inside my body.

If I didn't have one, I wouldn't be able to stand up. I'd be all floppy!

Our skeletons are made up of
lots of different bones. Big bones
and small bones join together.

Bones are very
hard and strong.

It is the joined bits of
our skeleton that move.

My knees and elbows bend because this is where two bones join together...

so do my fingers...

and my toes.

This is my backbone.

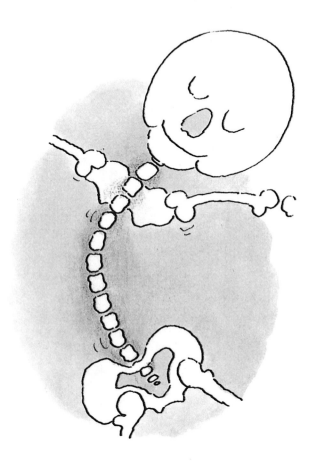

It is really lots of small bones joined
together so that it can bend.

My backbone goes all the way
from my head down my back
to my bottom.

My bones are all moved by muscles.

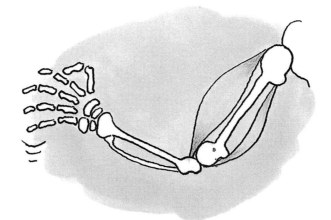

These are like big, stretchy elastic bands joined to the bones.

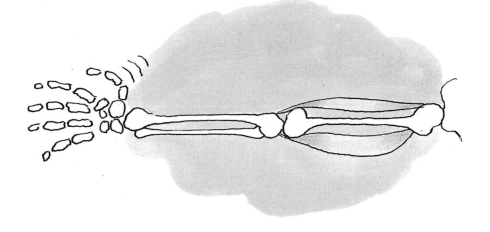

Muscles pull the bones
up and down when I
want to move them.

Lots of animals have skeletons like we do.

This is my dog Jess.

This is my goldfish Jaws.

Birds have skeletons, too.

This skeleton is just like
the one inside you or me.

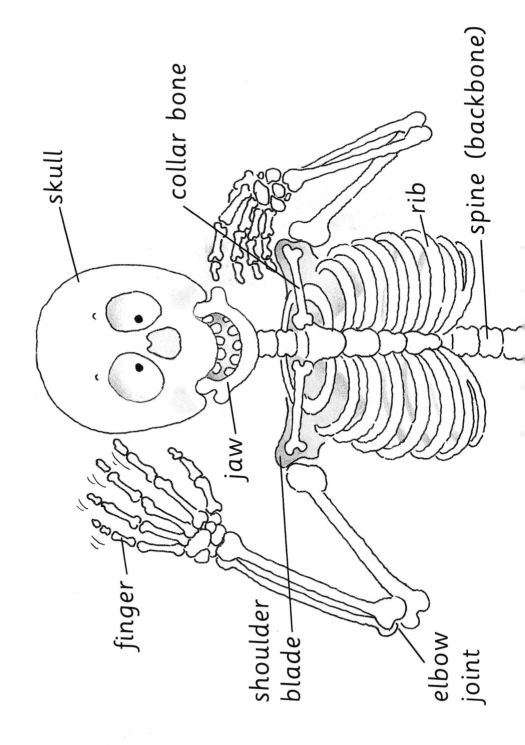

skull

collar bone

jaw

finger

shoulder
blade

elbow
joint

rib

spine (backbone)

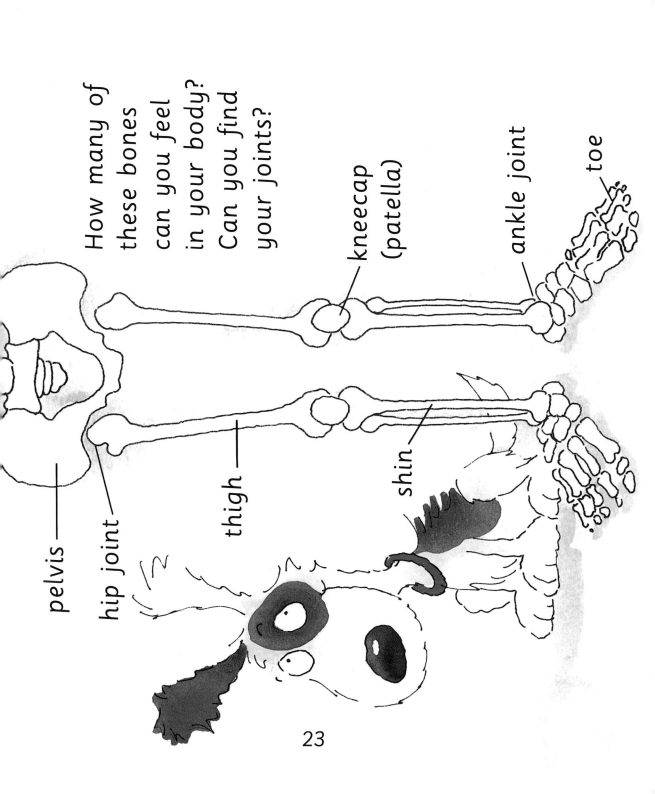

How many of these bones can you feel in your body? Can you find your joints?

pelvis

hip joint

thigh

kneecap (patella)

shin

ankle joint

toe

Notes for Adults

I'm Alive is a series of first information books particularly suitable for the early and emergent stages of reading.

Each book in the series includes simple, factual text, and amusing and colourful illustrations, to combine reading for pleasure with fact-finding.

The series takes a closer look at the human body and how it works and develops, comparing this with other forms of life. **I'm Alive** is designed to address the requirements of the National Curriculum for Science at key stage 1.

The books are equally suitable for use at school or at home. Below are some suggestions for extension activities that can be carried out with children to complement and extend the learning in this book.

Extension Activities

1 Make a cardboard skeleton. Use brass split pins to join the body parts and make the major joints. How many different joints are there in your body?

2 Make a poster about the different ways in which you can move your body. Cut out and collect pictures from magazines to stick on to your poster.

3 Move different parts of your body. Feel the muscles getting thinner and fatter as your bones move.

4 Imagine you couldn't move around on your own and had to use a wheelchair or crutches. How easy is it getting around your home or school?

5 Use mechano and elastic bands to build a model arm.